# Banyan

## Is a Very Special Coyote

# Banyan
## Is a Very Special Coyote

### Karen Edgerton

**walladog**
*publishing*

The content associated with this book is the sole work and responsibility of the author. Gatekeeper Press had no involvement in the generation of this content.

Banyan Is a Very Special Coyote

Published by Walladog publishing

Copyright © 2023 by Karen Edgerton

All rights reserved. Neither this book, nor any parts within it may be sold or reproduced in any form or by any electronic or mechanical means, including information storage and retrieval systems, without permission in writing from the author. The only exception is by a reviewer, who may quote short excerpts in a review.

The cover design, interior formatting, typesetting, and editorial work for this book are entirely the product of the author. Gatekeeper Press did not participate in and is not responsible for any aspect of these elements.

ISBN (paperback): 9781662947469

With Special Thanks to
Sheila and Scott

Not so long ago, on the dry western plains of the Great State of Texas, a litter of five baby coyotes is born.

The first thing Mama Coyote does is find her new family a home in a long-forgotten badger den.
She knows it will keep her little ones warm, dry, and most importantly, safe.
Sadly, Mama is the only parent now, and she worries about safety a lot.

FYI: Native to North America, coyotes are smart, resilient, and typically mate for life.

When the pups are just over two weeks old, Mama Coyote gives each young'un a name to guide them as they become grown adults.
It is Mama's dream that her offspring will grow to display the true coyote heart.

She names the pups: Star & Sprinter & Freedom & Tuffy.

FYI: Coyote pups are taught by their parents to hunt, recognize dangers, and socialize with others.

The 5th little female coyote is the smallest of the litter. But Mama knows that size is never the measure of a heart nor of a coyote's courage.

Mama Coyote raises her paw and says, "You are Banyan, named after the special tree whose roots reach out to the whole world."

FYI: The Banyan tree's branches grow roots of their own so one tree can spread out a long way, substantially impacting its environment.

Spring passes and summer begins.
Every morning the sun rises in the east and each night it sets in the west.

In the brightness of the day, the exuberant pups play, explore the scrub around their den, and learn the skills they need when grown and on their own.

At night, when the sky is black, Mama Coyote leaves them deep in the den, huddled in sleep, as she hunts far and wide for the food to keep her youngsters' bellies full.

FYI: Coyotes frequently feed on carrion, such as deer on the side of the road, thus helping to keep the environment clean and healthy.

It is early in the morning, before the sun appears in the sky, that Mama Coyote always comes back with a feast for her growing pups to eat.

But one morning, when the sun is already risen, the young coyotes awake to find Mama Coyote is not back home.

FYI: Coyotes are most often killed by man through hunting (84%) and collisions with vehicles (14%)

"Mama, mama, where are you mama," the anxious pups cry throughout the day and long into the night.
But still Mama Coyote does not return to them.
Exhausted, they fall into a deep and dreamless sleep.

The following day, Mama Coyote still had not come back to the den.
Frightened and confused, the half-grown pups realize they must now leave their home to survive.
They will need to follow Mama into the far and wide.

FYI: Coyotes can travel up to 100 miles to find food, but typically only go two to three miles in a day.

Gathering all they will need, the young coyotes, tears in their eyes, say goodbye to one another and set out to find their own way on the great western plains.

Little Banyan is the last to begin the long and arduous journey to find Mama Coyote.
She walks, under the blazing sun, through the prickly scrub, and over the crumbling dirt.
But where she is going, she doesn't know.

FYI: Coyote littermates often stay together for several years after weaning. Females may remain when grown with their mother's pack.

For two whole days Banyan walks in the heat of the sun, stopping only to drink what water she comes across and eat the few insects she finds.
At night, she sleeps on the rough, cold ground.

On the third day, suffering from both thirst and great hunger, she comes to the edge of a field covered with rusted metal pens and monstrous animals that bellow upon seeing her.

FYI: A cow can be over 50 times larger than the average coyote.

In fear of the large, noisy animals, Banyan turns to run back the way she came.

But at that moment, a huge red truck comes hurtling toward her, with a deafening sound and angry dust swirling all around it.

Diving under the nearest pen, Banyan hides amongst the bellowing herd.

FYI: Coyotes hate loud noises like horns as well as bright flashing lights. Smells such as ammonia, mothballs, vinegar and pepper also deter them.

Although the feedlot is now dark and still, Banyan is not sure it is safe enough to move.

Then out of the night, she is startled to hear a low, rumbling voice above her.

"My but you are a tiny thing," the beast towering over her says, "You look like a coyote, but I think you are too small to be out on your own."

"I am not too small," Banyan replies, looking up defiantly, "And I can take care of myself. Because I am a coyote!"

FYI: Adult coyotes can range in size from 15 to 40 pounds with the males being larger.

"Well," the huge animal says softly now, "I am a cow, and you are in the feedlot we call home. You are welcome to stay here as long as you like."

Banyan looks up, sensing kindness in the voice and smiles for the first time in days.

It takes several weeks, but the feedlot doesn't seem so bad once Banyan gets used to it.

There are lots of places for her to hide plus many other small creatures that come to forage for food and keep her company.

FYI: Feedlots are fenced areas of land that are estimated to produce about 97% of the beef consumed in the US.

Soon, Banyan discovers there are also two special animals who will find a lasting place in her heart.

There is Gus the grackle, with huge wings of black and a very loud squawk.

And the fat orange cat, Chester, who claims the humans on the lot feed him until his belly hurts.

There are also the silent foxes, the grumpy skunks and the chatty raccoons who won't give their names but always speak of somewhere else they have to be.

FYI: Grackles are a variety of blackbird and responsible for dispersing thousands of pounds of seeds each year in their waste products.

Banyan enjoys them all, although some only from a distance, but Gus and Chester are her true friends.
The monstrous cows, as nice as they are, do not stay long enough at the feedlot to get to know.

Day after day, Banyan, Gus and Chester are together. They play games in the cool of the morning, nap in the afternoon heat and hunt for food at nightfall.

FYI: Temperatures in west Texas can be above 100 degrees for days in the summer while winter temperatures are below 65 degrees.

Settling into her new home, Banyan makes her den in an abandoned building and over time, explores every corner of the many acres of the lot.

She finds grain silos with plentiful insects to eat and hidden places the humans throw unwanted food. She digs up wild onions in the long grass and eats new plant shoots when she can.

FYI: Coyotes primarily eat a diet of small mammals, amphibians and insects. However, they will also consume plant matter when hungry.

Although life is quite difficult. time moves very quickly on the lot.

One after another the days gather into weeks and the weeks line up into months.

Before she even realizes it, Banyan has lived at the feedlot for almost two whole years.

FYI: Animals rely on an internal 24-hour cycle called a circadian rhythm. They also look to the amount of daylight present. Coyote families will gather in the morning at sunrise to play and socialize.

It is a good life; Banyan often thinks as she lies in the shade of the broken-down trucks during the hot afternoon sun.

But more importantly, she thinks, it is her life.
And although Banyan remembers what Mama Coyote wished for her when she was given her name, she is still proud to be a strong and resilient coyote.

FYI: Coyotes live 10-14 years in the wild but can live much longer in a zoological setting, sometimes up to 20 years.

Sadly however, what Banyan doesn't know, is that she is slowly starving.

Chester teases her about how thin she is, but the naive coyote thinks it is just said to be silly. And Gus often gives her the insects he needs to eat.

Banyan can't see that fur no longer covers the bones showing beneath her skin.

She becomes used to scratching constantly and not being able to run as far as she could just months before.

Hunger gnaws at her daily, but it is the way it is now and she does not think much about it.

FYI: Animals that eat plants are herbivores, animals that eat meat are carnivores, and an animal that eats both plants and meat is an omnivore.

Then one day, a human appears Banyan has never seen.
There are always humans on the feedlot, but they throw rocks at her, and she both fears and tolerates them.

This human though, is different.
Its smell makes Banyan feel calm.
When it talks out loud, the coyote's heart beats a little faster and her stomach flutters.
Completely unprepared, Banyan suddenly feels her life is about to change.

FYI: Pheromones are a chemical substance produced by an animal that will attract its own species and repel other species.

Walking along the paths Banyan herself travels daily, the new human periodically stops to look in each building or container with obvious interest.
Confused, but also very excited, the silent coyote follows like a ghost.

FYI: It is thought a coyote can smell a predator, as well as a human, from over a mile away.

After a long time passes, the new human finishes their walk and slowly drives off the feedlot.
Banyan, suddenly sad, decides to head back to her den to lie down and think about these new feelings.

But as she rounds the corner of the abandoned building, she abruptly stops in amazement.

In front of her lies a magnificent feast.
In fact, there is more food spread out upon the ground than Banyan has ever even imagined.

FYI: Animals in the wild who must hunt for their food can never be certain when the next meal will be.

In front of her are plates of cooked meat and bowls of hot grains and a bucket of cool water.
Without understanding why, Banyan finds she cannot move and is filled with both longing and bewilderment.
Then she sees a glint of light and hears a sound - 'click'.

Her mind clouding with uncertain fear, Banyan runs from the food she so desperately needs until she is too exhausted to run any more.

FYI: Recommended foods for very hungry or sick canines included cooked chicken or hamburger plus boiled rice and canned pumpkin.

It isn't long before word about the feast spreads throughout the feedlot.

That night, after Gus and his crew eat their fill, the raccoons and skunks share a snack and Chester eats all he possibly can, Banyan returns and cautiously moves closer toward the food.

'Click'.

A picture of Banyan's ear appears on the tiny screen.

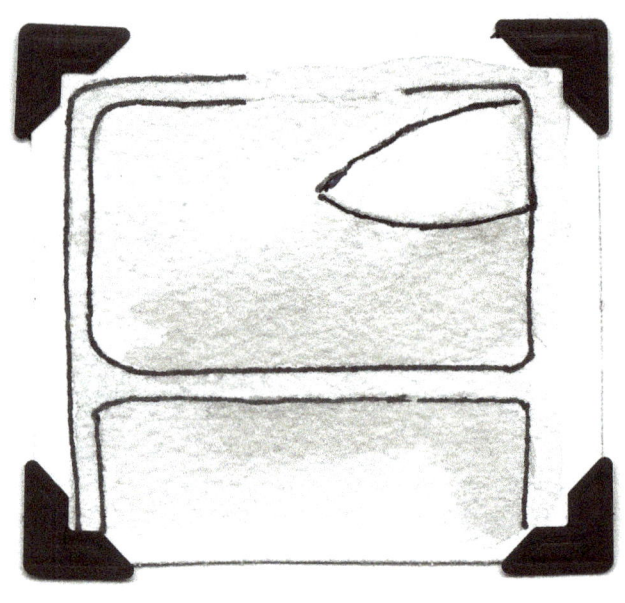

And far away, the visiting human watching through the lens, begins to cry.

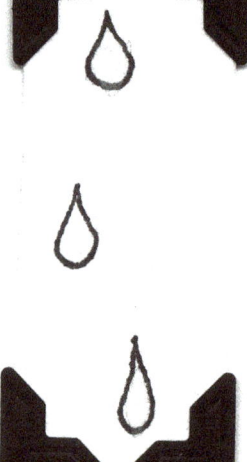

FYI: Like all wild creatures, coyotes are very distrustful of man.

When the hunger finally wins against the fear, Banyan begins to fill her belly with warm meat and buttery cooked rice.

She no longer hears the camera click each time she moves and continues to eat without another thought until the sun comes up.

She does, however, stop once, for just a moment, to look up to the sky and whisper a word of thanks.

FYI: An average coyote eats between 2 and 3 pounds of food each day.

The next day, the human comes again, and more plates of chicken and bowls of rice appear outside the abandoned building.

This time, without hesitation, Banyan eats her fill as soon as the new human leaves.
When she is done, the grackles and the foxes, the raccoons and the skunks, all come and soon every morsel of food is gone and those at the feedlot give thanks.

FYI: When food is plentiful, many animals in the wild will tolerate others eating at the same time.

On the third day, when Banyan sees My Human (as she thinks of it now) once more leaving plates and bowls of food, she wonders if there is a way to show her gratitude, to thank this wonderful human for giving what none has thought to do before.

An idea comes to her.
And it is with astonishment My Human stops before leaving the lot to watch as Banyan runs past and out the gate, a huge grin on the thankful coyote's face.

FYI: Coyotes can run up to 43mph when pursuing game or being pursued by a predator.

On the fourth day, the plates heaped with meat and the bowls full of grains and the buckets of cool water appear once again.

This time, the feedlot animals have been waiting and immediately rush to eat.

But there is something else that is left, something unexpected.
And now, outside Banyan's makeshift den –
is a wild animal trap.

FYI: A Live Animal Cage Trap is an all metal, open-grid cage with a spring-loaded door that only closes when the animal is safely inside.

Banyan knows what a trap is, its grid of wire and snap close door is all too familiar.
She has watched both foxes and raccoons caught and carried off in them.
Banyan herself is much too smart to be fooled by a meager piece of bread or meat.


This trap, however, feels different.
She can smell My Human on it and on the cloth laying inside it.
Warily, Banyan circles the trap slowly, wondering what it means.

FYI: Coyotes can detect the slightest scent from a human on any object.

Without warning, Gus flies down and perches on the trap with a loud squawk.
He waves at Banyan with his large black wing.
"We must talk little friend. You must decide to go inside the trap. It belongs to the human who has been feeding you. And I believe this human will be a mother to you as Mama Coyote was."

In their time together, Gus has listened to many Mama stories, and from experience, he knows how to read the human heart.

FYI: Coyotes will recognize their parents even years after being apart.

Banyan stares at the trap, her heart racing with uncertainty.

Gus speaks again, "You must go in, my friend. You are starving now and will not survive much longer."

Then Gus wraps his great wing around the coyote as she begins to cry.

FYI: Current research shows that mammals, especially canines like coyotes, experience emotions like fear, happiness, anger, shame & love.

Memories of Mama Coyote come while Banyan tosses in her sleep.
Mama repeats what Gus has said and deep in her soul Banyan knows what is true.
She is starving and will not live through the coming summer heat.

In her sadness, Banyan cries aloud.
She loves her friends and knows she will miss them terribly and though the feedlot has become her home, she has often dreamed of a better place, a safer place.
This may be the only chance she has to save herself.

FYI: Scientists now agree the majority of mammals dream when they sleep. This has been confirmed by limb movement and by REMs or Rapid Eye Movements.

So, when the sweltering afternoon heat gives way to the cool air of the evening, Banyan makes the difficult decision.

With a last look back, she leaves the old building that has been her home for over two years and walks through her fear and into the trap.

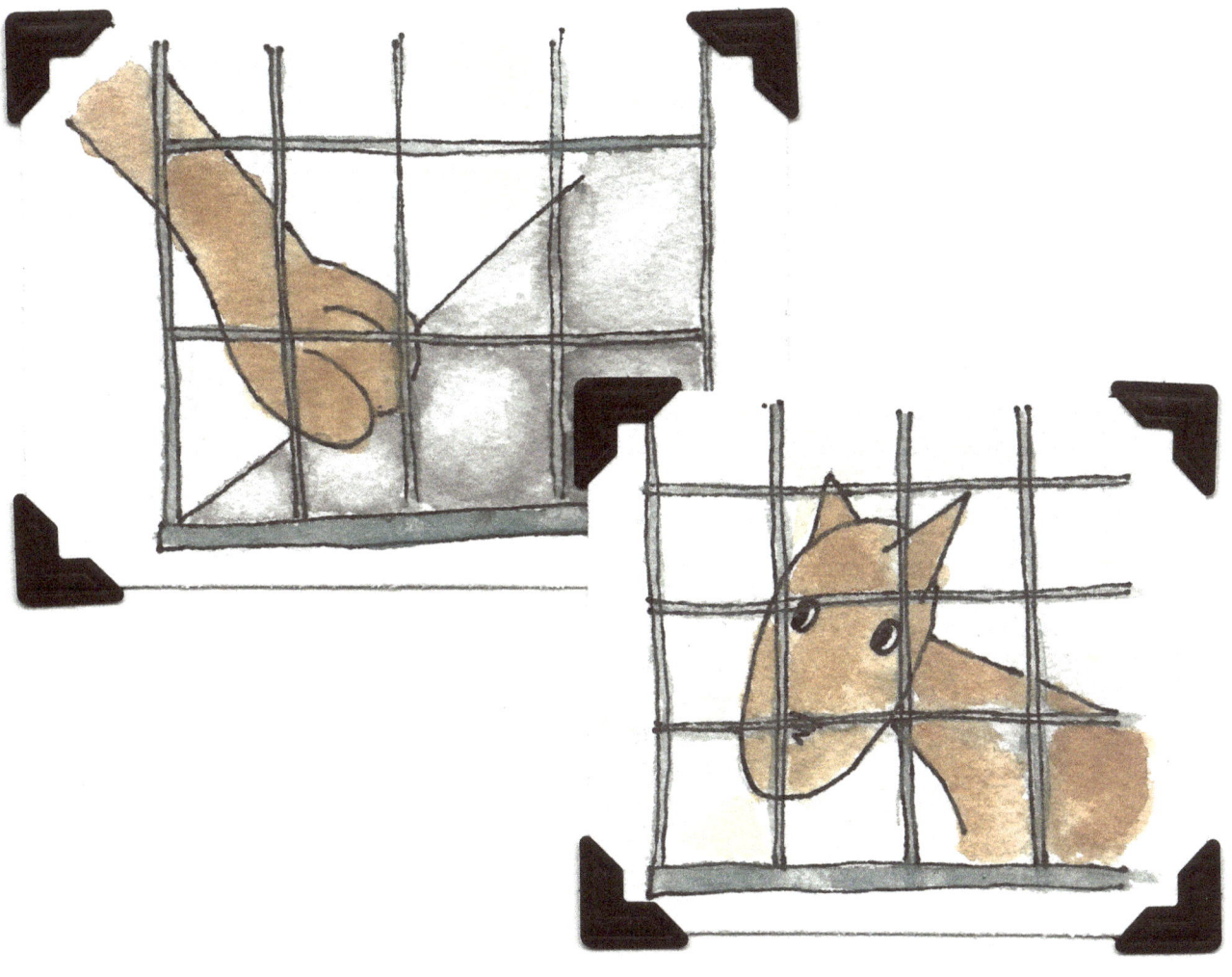

FYI: It can take several days to a week or more for a wild animal to go into a trap, if it will go in at all.

What happens next is a mixture of human hands and soft voices and the calm presence of My Human's smell.
Banyan is lifted up, still in the trap, and carried off in the kind of truck she has always feared.
Yet, she isn't filled with hate or anger or fear now.
She is soothed by the swaying movement, comforted by the cool air blowing on her body, and encouraged by the constant voice of My Human.

Without any doubt, Banyan knows, deep in her heart, an epic journey has begun.

FYI: Any animal, wild, stray or a lost pet, will experience a high level of stress when trapped and must be transported as soon as possible.

Night is fallen when Banyan comes to a large pen surrounded by the sounds and smells of unfamiliar things. Still, she is unafraid.

My Human has never left her side.

A waterproof tarp hangs atop the pen, attached to a tree with branches that reach into the sky.

A kennel where Banyan can hide from the overwhelming newness of everything waits for her in the corner.

Banyan sinks into a deep, restless sleep and as her eyes close, she knows what she feels is joy.

FYI: Coyotes living near human populations will sleep during the day and are most active at night. In the wild, they sleep at night while hunting and socializing during the day.

In the first days of Banyan's new life, she does little but eat until her belly aches then falls asleep and does not dream.

My Human comes many times a day, replacing empty plates with full ones and talking softly all the while.

Banyan doesn't understand what is said, but the sound calms her and continues to put her at ease.

FYI: With time and training, animals can learn certain human words. But the tone used can produce an immediate positive or negative reaction.

A week passes and Banyan begins to heal.
She gains weight from the daily feasts of cooked chicken and rice, and the cool water from the over-flowing bucket hydrates her.
She relaxes on the dry straw covering the pen floor and naps under the shade of the tarp.
Gradually, she feels her strength returning.

My Human comes many, many times a day.
And when it does, Banyan breathes in its smell and breathes out all her worries.

FYI: Pheromones are signature chemicals animals produce that attract their own kind and repel other species.

One morning, to her surprise, Banyan wakes to a loud cackling voice and for a moment believes Gus has followed her to her new home.

She sits up and looks around.

Astonished, she finds a big red bird talking in rhyme.

"I know who you are, you came very far, in a cage in a car, must feel so bizarre!"

Banyan, her jaw hanging open, stands rooted to the ground.

FYI: Researchers have found 12 common, and specific, sounds chickens make that have different meanings.

"Don't worry," a low, scratchy voice says. "It takes her a day to think those up. I'm Tater Tot. I'm a pig. That's Hanna, she's a chicken. And you are?"
Banyan replies enthusiastically, "I'm a coyote! I don't know what a pig is, but the noisy one is a bird."

FYI: Predators and prey in the wild seldom form beneficial relationships, while domestic animals of different species frequently live in harmony.

Then, as anyone who knew them could have predicted, before the day is done, Hanna the big red chicken, Tater Tot the pig and Banyan the coyote become the fastest of friends.

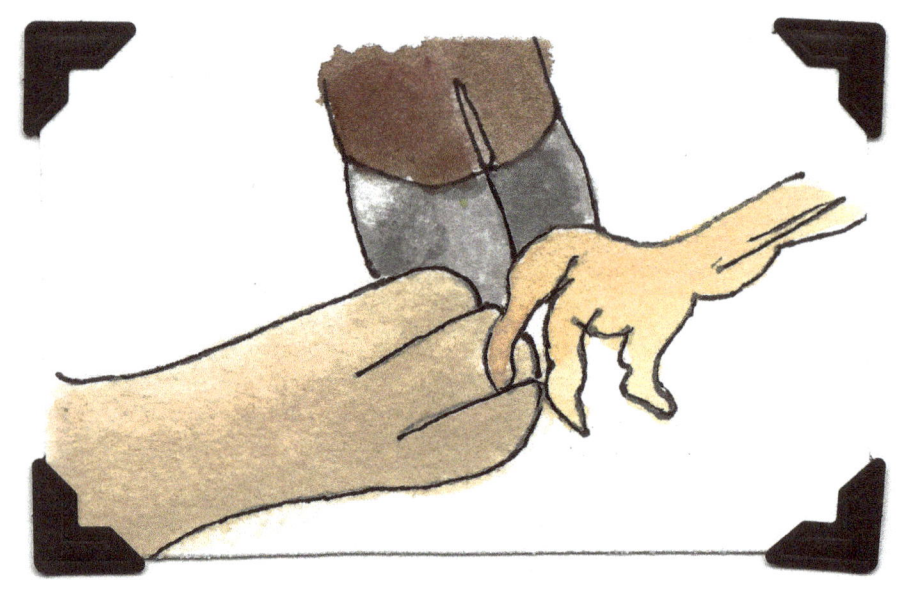

In their effort to help her feel at home, Hanna continues cackling loudly when she can't think of words to rhyme, and Tater Tot states he will answer every question Banyan has.

FYI: Pigs defend against predators with intense, high-pitched screams if threatened.

"Where am I? Why does My Human smell like sunshine? Why do my ears tickle? Is that box my new den?" Banyan blurts out to Tater Tot the next morning.
"Slow down young coyote," the pig says, "I will tell you all you need to know."

"First, you are in a safe place with two exceptionally kind humans. Second, My Human, as you call her, is a female, and they smell wonderful," Tater Tot says looking up to the sky with a smile.

FYI: Pigs are known to have at least 20 different vocalizations with varied meanings.

Later in the day, Tater Tot takes a deep breath, waves his hoof at Hanna to quiet down, and continues answering Banyan's questions.

"The box is called a kennel and yes, you are supposed to use it as a den," he says.

"And your ears tickle because your fur is starting to grow back, and it is growing back quickly!"

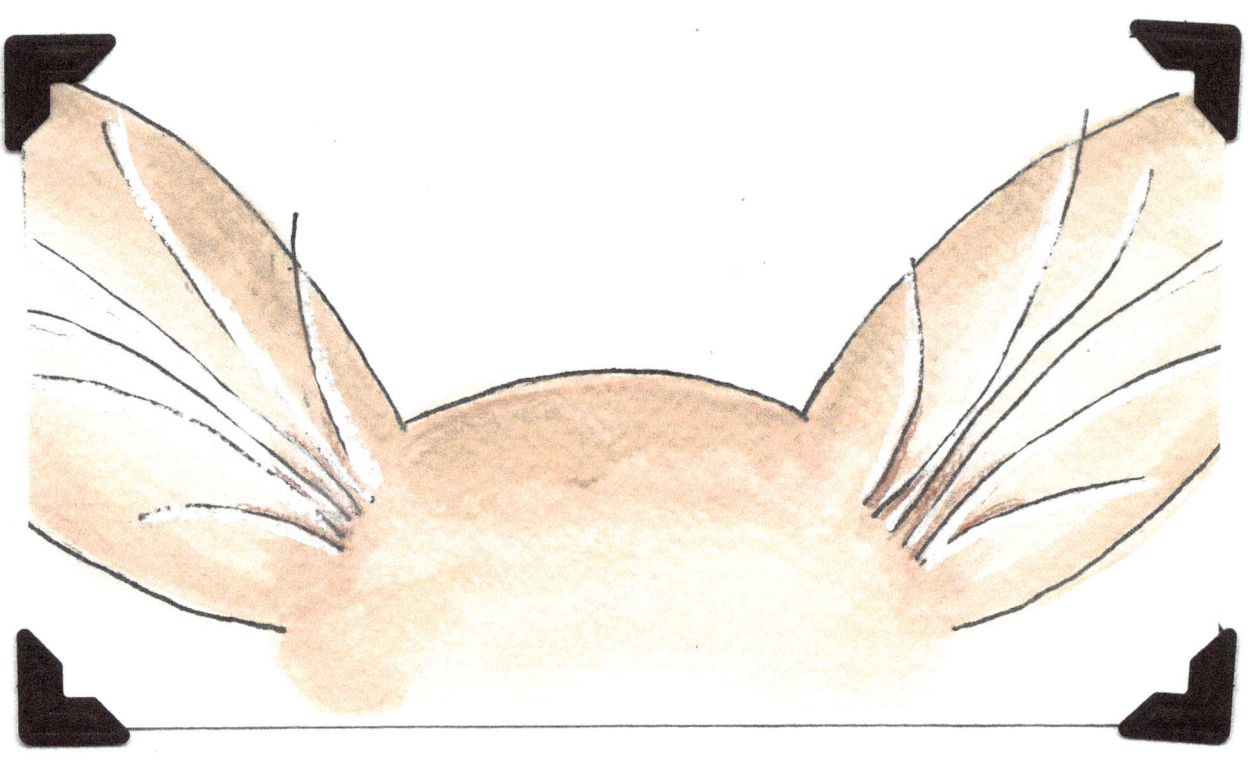

FYI: Mammals have hair in their ears that capture sound vibrations. Coyotes can hear vocalizations up to three miles away on a clear night.

Every day begins the same.
My Human comes to see Banyan with food and fresh water, then stays and talks until the sun is high in the sky.

Then Hanna arrives and cackles for hours, trekking back and forth along the top rail of the pen.
"You look very good, with all you eat, you really should," the chicken squawks out loud the morning of day twenty-six under My Human's dedicated care.
"I agree Hanna." Banyan replies.
"I feel much better. Have you seen Tator Tot?" she asks, trying to divert the noisy chicken.
"I have not, seen Tater Tot, but I will look, in every nook," she answers, hopping down from her perch.

FYI: Traditionally, coyotes are natural predators to chickens.

In no time at all, Banyan feels at home.
The pen is smaller than the feedlot, but it is more comfortable, there is more to eat, and a feeling of love is present that this coyote never thought possible.

And for fun, Banyan, the smart girl she is, soon finds that she can control making the camera go 'click'.

FYI: Coyote communication occurs mainly by eye contact, facial expressions, and body language. It is subtle and usually just understood by other coyotes.

Then one night, when the dark sky above her pen is lit with the pinpoints of distant stars and her heart is filled with joy, Banyan starts to dance.

Caught on camera, My Human watches Banyan through the night, and feels their two hearts dancing as one.

FYI: The First People tell a story of how Coyote put the stars in the sky.

One day, a flock-mate of Hanna's decides to lay two eggs beside Banyan's pen.
Hiding them in the overflow of straw, no one notices the little eggs until the day they hatch.

FYI: Coyotes are considered opportunistic hunters and do not prey on other animals for sport, only for food. In recent years, human encroachment has diminished the natural food supply.

As the chicks become vocal and their peeps are heard near the pen, the humans come running.
Banyan, showing interest, moves in close, her nose sticking through the bars of the pen.
The newborn chicks have nothing to fear, she thinks, as she backs away after taking a quick look.
After, Banyan wonders why the humans were so afraid.

"Really," Banyan says to Tater Tot later in the day, "I thought they might like to get a ride on my head!"
The very wise pig stays silent and only smiles.

FYI: In October of 2008 the first YouTube video of a lioness that adopted a baby antelope spread through the Internet world.

Living in a pen instead of the feedlot limits her movement. It doesn't matter to Banyan at first because she was so ill, but now she feels better, and she thinks of how she used to run all night long.

The best part of the day is still when My Human comes to bring food or water or to sit beside her.

Once My Human stands away from the pen with two little humans.

They wave at Banyan, and she unexpectedly feels like the most special coyote on the planet.

FYI: Children between the ages of 2 and 7 have the greatest ability to learn of any other human on the planet.

Then just a few days later, My Human takes away the den and replaces it with one meant for travelling.

Banyan is confused by this and by the sadness she senses in My Human.

She worries she has done something wrong and decides she must discover what is happening.

FYI: The biggest factor in animal training is the level and kind of energy the human is experiencing. Animals can sense if humans are anxious, or fearful or confident and will react accordingly.

"Tater Tot," Banyan calls out later in the day, "can we talk? I... I think something is wrong."

"Of course," the concerned pig replies. "What's up?"

Her voice quivering, Banyan asks, "Why do I have a new kennel? Why is My Human so sad now? Am I doing something wrong?"

Tater Tot looks at the ground, then back up at Banyan.

As he speaks, a tear runs down his face.

"No Banyan, you are not doing anything wrong. But you are healthy and fit now and it is time for you to go and live in a better place with others like yourself," Tater Tot says softly.

FYI: Phenotypic plasticity is the process by which animals can adjust their behavior in response to a change in environment that also increases their fitness to thrive in that environment.

"This decision is made in love. You will go to live in a new pen, in a wonderful place, with lots of new friends," adds the pig, smiling now, his happiness for Banyan's new adventure showing.

Speechless, Banyan stands in silence.

Finally, she hesitantly asks, "Will I see My Humans again?"

Tater Tot grins widely and answers, "Of course you will. As often as they can make the journey."

FYI: A wild animal that experiences domestication is not capable of being a pet nor being returned to its natural environment. Instead, a sanctuary or zoo is the best option.

The journey Banyan is preparing to make is equally very exciting and very sad.
Leaving My Human and the friends she made will be hard, but it is an important step for Banyan to take if she is going to be the Coyote Ambassador she was born to be.

Banyan doesn't know yet, but she is leaving for a new and forever home at The Austin Zoo in Austin, TX.
There she will be in a beautiful, large enclosure with lots of room to run and play and teach visiting humans what the heart of a coyote truly is.

We have been told Banyan's next-door neighbors will be a group of friendly female wolves.
I'm sure there will be a lot of talking over the fence!

FYI: If you are interested in supporting Banyan and
The Austin Zoo go to www.austinzoo.org.
The Austin Zoo is a 501C non-profit organization

Banyan when rescued at the feedlot.

Banyan today.

www.ingramcontent.com/pod-product-compliance
Lightning Source LLC
Chambersburg PA
CBHW042359070526
44585CB00029B/2995